MACHINES RULE!

ON THE
RACE TRACK

Steve Parker

Smart Apple Media

Smart Apple Media
P.O. Box 3263
Mankato, Minnesota 56002

Published by arrangement with the Watts Publishing
Group Ltd, London.

Library of Congress Cataloging-in-Publication Data

Parker, Steve, 1976-
  On the race track / Steve Parker.
      p. cm.—(Machines rule!)
  Includes bibliographical references and index.
  ISBN 978-1-59920-287-7 (hardcover)
  1. Motorsports—Juvenile literature. 2. Automobiles, Racing—
Juvenile   literature. I. Title.
  GV1019.2.P37 2010
  796.7–dc22

                                                2008044508

Editor: Jeremy Smith
Design: Billin Design Solutions
Art director: Jonathan Hair
Picture credits: Alamy: OFC main, 6, 8 all, 9tl, 13b, 13t, 26b,
27tr, 27b. Corbis: 7t, 14 all, 15c, 16tr, 17tl, 17tr, 17b, 20, 21c,
24, 25b, 25tr, 27tl. istockphoto: 7b, 10t, 21tl, 21tr, 25tl.
Shutterstock: OFC bl & br, 2, 3, 4, 7c, 9tr, 10b, 11 all, 12 all,
13tr, 15tr, 15b, 16b, 18, 19 all, 21 b, 22, 23 all, 26t.

Words in **bold** or ***bold italics*** can be found in the glossary on
page 28.

9 8 7 6 5 4 3 2 1

CONTENTS

They're Off!

At the race track, the final is about to begin. The engines roar and the drivers are tense and ready. The flag waves as the lights change and they're off! Lap after lap, the racers show their skills as they put their machines to the test. At the checkered flag, winner takes all!

F1 Car

Nothing is faster around a twisty track than a Formula One (F1) car. It brakes hard for the corner, then streaks away with a deafening whine. This vehicle is the ultimate racing machine. F1 is the richest, most famous, most glamorous racing in the world.

Rally Cars

Rally cars tackle any terrain, from smooth speedways to the roughest, bumpiest old tracks of gravel, sand, mud, and snow. The cars must be strong, sturdy, and reliable. The **navigator's** map-reading skills are vital—no one wants to get lost!

Motorcycles

Swap four wheels for two, and you're riding a top motocross motorcycle. Lean into the bend so your knees graze the track, then roar off down the straight. Keep the front wheel on the track—**wheelies** waste time!

Dragsters

From a standing start, no racing machine picks up speed as fast as the dragster. Each race is earsplitting and ground-shaking as two monster dragsters speed along the track. Both want to be first to flash past the finish line.

F1 Racecars

Formula One, or F1, is the best of the best. No other car can beat an F1 car for speed, handling, acceleration, braking, and all-round racing action. And F1 racing has more spectators than any other motor sport.

Up to 20 F1 **Grand Prix** races are held each year around the world. The races are about 186 miles (300 km) long and last up to two hours.

The driver's helmet has a radio in it that is used to talk to the team at the trackside.

During each race the cars go into the **pit** for new tires, a refill of fuel, and small repairs. It all takes less than 10 seconds!

Typical F1 car

Length: 14.7 ft (4.5 m)

Width: 5.9 ft (1.8 m)

Height: 3.1 ft (0.95 m)

Wheelbase: 10.1 ft (3.1 m)

Weight: 1,322 lbs (600 kg) on the start grid

Engine: 2.4 liters V8 (8 cylinder)

Power: 900-plus horsepower

Gears: 6 or 7, semi-automatic with paddle shift

Top speed: Over 199 mph (320 km/h)

THAT'S INCREDIBLE

During an F1 race, the driver loses more than 8 lbs (4 kg) of body weight, mainly as sweat.

Dozens of electronic sensors in the F1 car gather information, from tire pressure to how much fuel is left, and send it by radio to the team's many computers.

In North America, NASCAR races are the biggest. The National Association for Stock Car Auto Racing organizes contests around giant arenas, watched by some of the world's biggest crowds.

Stock cars have a roll cage inside the car that protects the driver if there's a crash.

Stock cars are specially made versions of everyday cars that ordinary people drive. They are modified for racing.

Stats and Facts

The driver watches the dials on the dashboard to check for problems.

THAT'S INCREDIBLE

NASCAR draws crowds of up to 180,000 people. Tens of millions watch on TV, and there are 75 million regular fans.

Crashes happen all the time in NASCAR racing.

Typical NASCAR Sprint Cup stock car

Length: 16.4 ft (5 m)

Width: 6.2 ft (1.9 m)

Height: 4.9 ft (1.5 m)

Wheel base: 9.1 ft (2.8 m)

Weight: 1.7 tons (1.5 t) with driver

Fuel tank: 17.7 gallons (67.2 L)

Engine: 5.8 L V8 (8 cylinder)

Power: More than 750 horsepower

Gears: 4-speed manual

Top speed: 199 mph (320 km/h)

Track length: .5 miles–2.5 miles (805 m–4,023 m)

Rally Cars

Drivers roar up hills and often take off at the top. →

THAT'S INCREDIBLE

The longest, hardest motor race is the Dakar Rally. It runs from European cities all the way through African deserts.

Like stock cars, rally cars are souped-up versions of ordinary cars. But rallying takes place off-road. Drivers cope with lumps, bumps, mud, dirt, streams, snow, ice, and much more for three or four days!

Rally cars have **Four Wheel Drive (4WD)**, giving the cars great grip to the ground.

Stats and Facts

The driver sits in the left seat and the navigator in the right seat. They are strapped in tight, and everything in the car is well padded.

The World Rally Championship (WRC) puts on about 15 races in Europe, South America, Australia, and New Zealand each year. Most are on dirt roads but a few are in snowy places such as Sweden and Norway.

Typical WRC car

Length: 14.1 ft (4.3 m)

Width: 5.9 ft (1.8 m)

Height: 4.9 ft (1.5 m)

Wheelbase: 8.5 ft (2.6 m)

Weight: At least 1.3 tons (1.2 t)

Engine: 2 liters turbocharged

Power: Up to 350 horsepower

Gears: Usually 5

Top speed: 124 mph (200 km/h)

Endurance Racing

To avoid getting tired, ordinary drivers should take a break every hour or two. Yet endurance car races run all day and all night—that's 24 hours at full speed!

The Le Mans 24-hour race has been taking place since 1923. ⟶

THAT'S INCREDIBLE

The tradition of the winning driver spraying the crowd with fizzy champagne began at Le Mans with Dan Gurney in 1967!

Audi R8 (five-time Le Mans winner)

Length: 15.2 ft (4.65 m)

Width: 6.5 ft (2.0 m)

Height: 4.1 ft (1.25 m)

Wheelbase: 8.9 ft (2.73 m)

Weight: 1 ton (911 kg)

Engine: 3.6 liters V8, twin turbo

Power: 600 horsepower

Gears: 6

Top speed: 211 mph (340 km/h)

Mechanics and engineers must be ready at any time for their car to come into the pit, even in the middle of the night.

Before the race, the car is taken apart, cleaned, and every tiny part is checked to make sure it will last for 24 hours nonstop.

MotoGP is the Motorcycle Grand Prix series. The bikes that race have amazing power and speed, breathtaking acceleration, heart-stopping brakes, and the best all-round performance.

Racing motorcyclists lean into bends, their knees almost touching the ground, as they take the fastest route or "racing line."

Racing motorbikes have *disc brakes*.

Stats and Facts

Colored flags are used in motor racing. A blue flag means a rider should let another racer pass, for example, if the opponent behind is more than a lap ahead of other racers.

Typical MotoGP bike such as Honda RC212V

Length: 6.7 ft (2.05 m)

Width: 2.1 ft (0.65 m)

Height: 3.7 ft (1.13 m)

Wheelbase: 4.7 ft (1.44 m)

Weight: 330 lbs (150 kg) basic

Fuel: 5.5 gallons (21 L)

Engine: Up to 800 cc (0.8 liters)

Power: 200 horsepower

Front wheels: 15 inches (406 mm) diameter

Rear wheels: 16 inches (419 mm) diameter

Top speed: 215 mph (347 km/h)

THAT'S INCREDIBLE

Moto GP races go distances of 60-80 miles (95–130 km) in as little as 40 minutes!

Riders wear strong crash helmets and tough leather suits for protection in crashes.

If you like dirt, mud, cold water, slips, slides, twists, bumps, and shakes, all with the noisy whine of a motorbike engine—then motocross is for you.

THAT'S INCREDIBLE
Some motocross races are for riders as young as four years of age!

The front wheel is held in **forks** that can slide upward as part of the **suspension**, to smooth out bumps and holes.

In motocross races, the tracks have steep slopes where riders take off and "fly" for long distances.

Typical Motocross MX1 motorcycle

Length: 7.2 ft (2.2 m)

Width: 2.6 ft (0.8 m)

Height: 3.9 ft (1.2 m)

Seat height: 3.3 ft (1 m)

Wheelbase: 5 ft (1.5 m)

Weight: 240 lbs (110 kg)

Engine: 250 cc 2-stroke or 450 cc 4-stroke

Gears: 5

Fuel: 1.6–1.8 gallons (6–7 L)

Top speed: 94 mph (152 km/h)

At the start, riders all roar off together.

Freestyle is a category where riders are judged on their jumps, stunts, tricks, and skills.

Dragsters

No race is as quick and loud as drag racing. There are only two cars each time, and they are in action for less than five seconds!

THAT'S INCREDIBLE

As the best dragsters blast past the finish line, they are going more than 329 mph (530 km/h)!

A drag race takes place on a straight track that's a quarter of a mile (402.3 m) long from start to finish.

The countdown at the start line is shown by a series of colored lights called a *Christmas Tree*.

Top Fuel Dragster

Category: Fastest type of dragster

Fuel: 9/10ths nitromethane, 1/10th methanol

Wheelbase: Up to 25 ft (7.6 m)

Height: Less than 7.5 ft (2.3 m) to top of wing

Weight: 2,205 lbs (1,000 kg)

Engine: Up to 2.2 gallons (8.2 L)

Power: More than 7,000 horsepower

Gears: 1

Top speed: Over 310 mph (500 km/h) at finish

There are several classes of dragster. Funny Cars look more like ordinary cars, but they still have massive back tires for super **acceleration**.

Dragster engines have superchargers on top.

Monster Trucks

For fun and thrills, as well as speed and power, why not visit the local speedway or racetrack when the monster trucks are in town?

THAT'S INCREDIBLE
Monster truck Bigfoot 14 did a long jump over a Boeing jet airliner!

Bigfoot trucks are specially built to look like normal pickup trucks but with massive tires. The first Bigfoot was built in 1975. Now there are more than 20 around the world, plus many similar-looking monster trucks.

Stats and Facts

Big racing trucks have 12-liter turbocharged diesel engines.

Drivers gain points for their skills, like performing wheelie stunts or for driving on the two wheels on the same side.

Pickup trucks modified for speed can reach more than 125 mph (200 km/h).

Bigfoot 17

Based on: Ford F150 Pickup Truck

Length: 18 ft (5.5 m)

Width: 12.5 ft (3.8 m)

Height: 10.2 ft (3.1 m)

Weight: 4.6 tons (4.2 t)

Engine: 11 liter Ford Racing V8

Power: 1,750 horsepower

Gears: 2

Tire height: 5.5 ft (1.67 m)

Top speed: 155 mph (250 km/h)

Many world champion racers started on the kart track. Go-karts are small and simple, but they are also fast and tricky to steer and brake. You need great skills to win a race.

Go-karts are like mini race cars, with an engine, gearbox, and four tiny wheels. They are so low that even when driving slowly, it seems like you are zooming at high speed.

THAT'S INCREDIBLE
The fastest types of go-karts, Superkarts, can reach speeds of 155 mph (250 km/h)—more than twice the highway speed limit!

The throttle (accelerator) pedal is on the right and the brake pedal on the left.

Drivers try to speed past on the straight and overtake on the inside at bends.

Stats and Facts

Typical KF1 (Formula A) kart

Length: Up to 5.9 ft (1.82 m)

Width: Up to 4.6 ft (1.4 m)

Height: Up to 2.1 ft (0.65 m) (excluding seat)

Wheelbase: 3.2 ft (1 m)

Weight: 176 lbs (80 kg)

Fully loaded: 343 lbs (156 kg) with driver

Fuel tank: 2.1 gallons (8 L)

Engine: 125 cc

Gears: Continuous change (no separate gears)

Transmission: Chain and sprocket

Suspension: None

Top speed: 87 mph (140 km/h)

Demolition Derby

Old cars, or "bangers," might rust away slowly in a junkyard. Or they might get crashed, smashed, crushed, and destroyed in a demolition derby!

THAT'S INCREDIBLE

The Chrysler Imperial from the mid-1960s is so tough and strong that it's banned from many demolition derbies because it would almost always win.

In the pit area, the cars are unloaded from their trailers. Most have already been in other derbies, or are already banged up.

Stats and Facts

Chrysler Imperial 1964–66

Length: 20.3 ft (6.2 m)

Width: 5.8 ft (1.78 m)

Height: 4.6 ft (1.4 m)

Weight: 2.2 tons (2 t)

Chassis: Extra-strong truck-type chassis

Bodywork: Wrap-around 'O' single steel sheet

Engine: Up to 7.2 liters

Top speed: 124 mph (200 km/h)

Survival is the key. Some drivers try to avoid crashes, while others aim to "take out" their rivals by ramming them into the fence.

The bodywork might get so bent in a crash that it rubs or cuts the tires. There's no time to lose—hit it with the sledgehammer!

Glossary

Acceleration
Picking up speed and going faster.

Christmas Tree
In motor sports such as drag racing, a group of colored lights that go on and off to count down to the start.

Disc brakes
Brakes that work by two pads, fixed to the vehicle, pressing on a ring-shaped disc that rotates with the road wheel.

Forks
On a motorcycle, the two bars or rods on either side of the front wheel, which hold it steady for steering and suspension.

Four-wheel drive (4WD)
When the engine turns all four wheels rather than just the front two or rear two.

Gears
A system of toothed cogs or gear wheels that come together or mesh in different combinations inside a gearbox, so a vehicle can go at different speeds for the same engine-turning speed.

Grand Prix
"Big Prize," one of the main events in sports like motor racing, especially Formula One (F1).

Navigator
In rally driving, the man or woman who sits next to the driver and reads out directions to them.

Pits
In motor racing, the garages and workshop areas where the cars are prepared for the race, and refuelled and repaired during the race.

Rally
In racing, when many people with the same kinds of vehicles gather to watch races.

Stock car
A make and model of car that is mass produced for ordinary driving, and which can be modified within certain rules for racing.

Supercharger
An add-on engine part that uses some form of air pump or fan compressor, driven directly by the engine, to force more air into the cylinders for extra power. Also called a "blower."

Suspension
The springs, pistons, levers, and other parts that soak up bumps and hollows in the ground, so the people in a vehicle have a smooth ride.

Turbocharged
An engine with an add-on engine part that uses exhaust gases to spin a fan-like turbine, which drives a compressor to force more air into the cylinders for extra power.

Wheelbase
The distance between the axles of a vehicle, from the center of the front wheel to the center of the back wheel.

Wheelie
When a vehicle rears up and its front wheels rise into the air, keeping the back ones on the ground.

Web Sites

http://www.speedace.info/formula_one.htm
All about Formula One (F1) racing, its history, the drivers, cars, and teams.

http://www.ducksters.com/sports/nascar.php
Learn about NASCAR drivers, cars, tracks, and what the technical words mean.

http://www.motorsport.com/photos
A huge collection of photos of almost all motor sports, from F1 to Champ Cars, rallying, motorcycles, and everything else.

http://www.karting.co.uk/Gallery/drivers/drivers-1.html
Photos of go-karting as part of the website of UK Karting, the official British go-karting organization.

Further Reading

Building a Stock Car (The World of NASCAR) by Will Deboard & Jim Gigliotti, Child's World, 2008

Dirt Bikes (Cool Rides) by Jack David, Bellwether, 2008

NASCAR (Eyewitness Books) by James Buckley, DK Children, 2005

Racecars (Up Close) by Andra Serlin Ambramson, Sterling, 2008

Note to Parents and Teachers:

Every effort has been made by the publishers to ensure that the web sites in this book are suitable for children, that they are of the highest educational value, and that they contain no inappropriate or offensive material. However, because of the nature of the Internet, it is impossible to guarantee that the contents of these sites will not be altered. We strongly advise that Internet access is supervised by a responsible adult.

Index